Yellow Umbrella Books are published by Capstone Press
151 Good Counsel Drive, P.O. Box 669, Mankato, Minnesota 56002
www.capstonepress.com

Printed in the United States of America

Library of Congress Cataloging-in-Publication Data
Ring, Susan.
The ocean / by Susan Ring.
p. cm.
Summary: A very simple introduction to the ocean, the plant and animal life within it, and how people use it.
ISBN 0-7368-2920-2 (hardcover)—ISBN 0-7368-2879-6 (softcover)
1. Ocean—Juvenile literature. [1. Ocean. 2. Ocean ecology. 3. Ecology.] I. Title.
GC21.5.R56 2004
551.46—dc21 2003008401

Editorial Credits
Editorial Director: Mary Lindeen
Editor: Jennifer VanVoorst
Photo Researcher: Wanda Winch
Developer: Raindrop Publishing

Photo Credits
Cover: Creatas; Title Page: Georgette Douwma/PhotoDisc; Page 2: Royalty-Free/Corbis; Page 3: PhotoLink/PhotoDisc; Page 4: Royalty-Free/Corbis; Page 5: DigitalVision; Page 6: DigitalVision; Page 7: Georgette Douwma/PhotoDisc; Page 8: Steven Haddock/ MBARI; Page 9: DigitalVision; Page 10: Brandon Cole/Visuals Unlimited; Page 11: Dotte Larsen/Bruce Coleman, Inc.; Page 12: Ron Chapple/ Thinkstock; Page 13: Royalty-Free/Corbis; Page 14: Royalty-Free/Corbis; Page 15: DigitalVision; Page 16: Creatas

1 2 3 4 5 6 09 08 07 06 05 04

The Ocean

by Susan Ring

Consultant: Steven Haddock, PhD, Scientist,
Monterey Bay Aquarium Research Institute

Yellow Umbrella Books

an imprint of Capstone Press
Mankato, Minnesota

Most of the Earth is covered with salty water. This water is called the ocean.

The ocean can be calm.
It can also have big waves.

Many plants grow in the ocean.
Kelp grows in underwater forests.

Many animals live in the ocean, too.

Whales and dolphins live in the ocean.

Many kinds of fish live in the ocean, too.

Some animals live in the deep water where it is dark.

Some animals live in coral reefs.

Other animals live where the ocean meets the land.

In some places, the ocean is very cold.

In other places, the ocean is very warm.

People use the ocean in many ways. People catch fish in the ocean.

People study animals that live in the ocean.

People swim in the ocean, too.
They play on its beaches.

Have you seen the ocean?

Words to Know/Index

beach—an area of sand or small rocks where land meets water; page 15

calm—quiet and peaceful; the ocean is calm when there are few waves and little wind; page 3

coral reef—a strip of rock made up of the hardened skeletons of corals; corals are small sea creatures that are many colors; page 9

dolphin—a smart water mammal with a long snout; a dolphin is smaller than a whale; page 6

Earth—the planet we live on; page 2

kelp—a kind of large seaweed; page 4

salty—full of salt; ocean water has salt and other minerals in it; salt water is not safe for people to drink; page 2

wave—a moving ridge on the surface of water; page 3

whale—a large sea animal that looks like a fish; a whale is a mammal and breathes air; page 6

Word Count: 139
Early-Intervention Level: 11